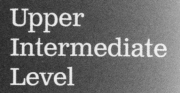
Bonjour, Piano!

ISBN 978-1-4950-8869-8

DURAND SALABERT ESCHIG
Editions Musicales

Visit Hal Leonard Online at
www.halleonard.com

CONTENTS

Editorial suggestions in the music appear in brackets.

COMPOSER BIOGRAPHIES

CLAUDE DEBUSSY
(1862-1918)

Claude Debussy was one of the most brilliant and important composers of the late-19th and early-20th centuries. His compositions had a profound effect on the composers that followed him, particularly owing to a new style of music that he helped create along with his contemporary, Maurice Ravel. Characteristics of this style included tonal centers rather than clear key associations, the use of whole-tone and other exotic scales, prolific use of parallel chords, and a deliberate ambiguity of rhythm, or lack of a clear rhythmic pulse. The impressionist movement in music implied generous reference to literature and art within musical compositions, exemplified by Debussy's many fancifully titled works such as the *Préludes, Estampes* and *Images* for piano. Debussy was trained as a pianist, but was not considered to be an outstanding player by the faculty at the Paris Conservatoire where he studied, so he did not pursue a concert career. He wrote music for the piano throughout his life, and ironically contributed some of the most important French works in the modern concert repertoire, as well as a proliferation of student pieces.

DARIUS MILHAUD
(1892-1974)

Darius Milhaud was a noted member of Les Six, a group of composers whose music was perceived as a reaction to both French Impressionism and extended Romanticism. His extremely large output of music (his opus list ended at 443) bears influences from both American jazz and Brazilian dance music. Like many other composers featured in this publication, he studied at the Paris Conservatoire. From 1917 to 1919, he worked as secretary to Paul Claudel, a poet and playright who also happened to be the French ambassador to Brazil. Milhaud and Claudel collaborated on many artistic projects, and the contact also allowed him the opportunity to travel to Brazil and become inspired by the popular music he heard there. Two significant works resulted from this experience: *Le boeuf sur le toit* (1920), a ballet full of Brazilian tunes, and *Saudades do Brasil* (1920), a piano suite of dances inspired by neighborhoods in Rio de Janeiro. Likewise, a 1922 trip to the United States, where Milhaud heard jazz in Harlem, provided the inspiration for the ballet suite *La creation du monde* (1923). Milhaud married his cousin Madeleine and they had a child. The Nazi invasion of France prompted them to flee to the United States in 1940. He began teaching at Mills College in Oakland, where his students included jazz pianist Dave Brubeck. After the war he was able to return to Paris and resume teaching at the Conservatoire until his retirement.

FRANCIS POULENC
(1899-1963)

A member of Les Six, Poulenc was born into a wealthy family of pharmaceutical manufacturers in Paris. He attended the Lycée Condorcet, a secondary school, instead of entering a conservatory. In Poulenc's early explorations of music, Debussy, Schubert, and Stravinsky made especially large impressions. His mother, an amateur pianist, gave him lessons from age 5 to 16, when he began formal studies with Ricardo Viñes. Poulenc's mother died that year, and his father died two years later. Viñes now became more of a mentor, and encouraged Poulenc to compose. He also helped Poulenc to meet the composers Auric and Satie. After serving in the French army from 1918 to 1921, Poulenc began composition lessons with Charles Koechlin. He also became an accompanist to baritone Pierre Bernac, who would later premiere many of Poulenc's art songs. A devout Catholic, Poulenc composed several sacred choral works, including a Mass in G, *Stabat Mater*, and *Gloria*. He also composed operas, ballets, film scores, orchestral pieces, chamber music, art songs, and piano music. In 1936 his composer friend Pierre-Octave Ferroud was killed in a particularly violent car accident, and this caused Poulenc to take a pilgrimage to the commune of Rocamadour, which contains some of the oldest churches in France. Following this journey, he brought a new seriousness and depth of religious feeling to his compositions. The most notable feature of Poulenc's music is his true gift for melody. Even his non-vocal works abound with fresh tunes, and these are paired with sensitive harmonic turns that carry his unique stamp.

PIERRE SANCAN
(1916-2008)

After early piano studies in Morocco and Toulouse, Sancan moved to Paris and studied with Yves Nat at the Conservatoire. He won several awards for his skills in composition and counterpoint, including the prestigious Prix de Rome in 1943 for his cantata *La Légende de Icare*. He achieved a teaching post at the Conservatoire in 1956, when Yves Nat retired. As a pianist, Sancan was highly regarded, though most of his public appearances were accompanying the cellist André Navarra. Sancan's compositions include an opera *Ondine* (1962), two ballets, two piano concertos, and advanced pieces for piano.

ERIK SATIE
(1866-1925)

One of the most eccentric personalities in all of music, Satie began piano studies in 1874, with a teacher who instilled a love of medieval music and chant. He entered the Paris Conservatoire in 1878, and was expelled two and a half years later for lack of talent. He was readmitted in 1885, but did not change the minds of his professors. After a detour in the Infantry – seen for a moment as a better career choice – Satie settled in the artistic Paris neighborhood of Montmartre in 1887. There he composed his first pieces: *Ogives*, for piano, written without barlines (a compositional choice found frequently in Satie's music) and the famous *Gymnopédies*. In 1890, while pianist and conductor at the cabaret Le Chat Noir, he met Claude Debussy and joined the spiritual movement Rose-Croix du Sâr Péladan (Rosicrucian Order), eventually becoming a choirmaster for the group. His involvement inspired the works *Sonneries de la Rose+Croix* and *Le Fils des Etoiles*. He had a brief and passionate relationship with the painter Suzanne Valadon in 1893. Brokenhearted after Suzanne left, he wrote *Vexations*, a theme to be played 840 times in a row – about twenty hours. In 1895 Satie abandoned his usual red robe and replaced it with seven identical mustard velvet suits, nicknaming himself "the Velvet Gentleman." In the next few years he moved to the suburb of Arcueil, and began taking composition lessons at the Schola Cantorum. He met Jean Cocteau, with whom he collaborated on the ballet *Parade* in 1916. Satie gradually met more artists of the French avant-garde, and presided over the birth of the group "Les Six." He died in 1925 of cirrhosis of the liver – probably due to his abundant consumption of absinthe. His friends visited his room in Arcueil – to which he had denied access throughout his life – and they discovered the state of poverty in which Satie had always lived.

HENRI SAUGUET
(1901- 1989)

Born Henri-Pierre Poupard, he used his mother's maiden name Sauguet when he began concertizing, to avoid embarrassing his father with activities in modern music. He studied the piano from an early age, and in 1916 became organist and choirmaster at Floirac near Bordeaux, taking organ lessons with Paul Combes. He studied composition first with Joseph Canteloube and later with Charles Koechlin. In his early career he met other notable composers such as Satie and Milhaud. Sauguet was a noted opera composer, with *La chartreuse de Parme* (1939) his largest-scale work in this vein. He composed several others over the course of his career, and for his first, *Le plumet du colonel* (1924), he even wrote the libretto. Sauguet also found success writing ballets, including *Les forains* (1945), about a traveling circus troupe. During the war, Sauguet used his status to help his many Jewish friends, while still producing an impressive amount of music, including his *Symphonie expiatoire* (1945), dedicated to the innocent victims of the war. Aside from composition, Sauguet was active as a critic for the French journals *L'Europe nouvelle, Le jour*, and *La bataille*. In 1976 he was elected to the Académie des Beaux-Arts in succession to Milhaud. He served as President of several organizations, among them the Union des Compositeurs, which he founded.

DÉODAT DE SÉVÉRAC
(1872-1921)

Sévérac was born in the former Languedoc region of France. He studied with Vincent d'Indy and Albéric Magnard at the Schola Cantorum in Paris, and later worked as an assistant to the Spanish composer Isaac Albéniz. He spent the remainder of his life in southern France. His opera *Héliogabale*, which included parts for some of the folk musicians from his beloved rural provinces, was produced at Béziers in 1910. Sévérac is noted for writing vocal and choral music that included settings of verse in the Provençal and Catalan languages. He wrote several collections of piano miniatures, including *Chant de la terre*, *En Languedoc*, and *En vacances*. His thesis at the Schola Cantorum, *La centralization et les petites chapelles en musique*, concerned the future of French music; he argued strongly for French composers to draw upon regional folk music sources to protect against the impact of foreign musical influences. Shortly before his death, Sévérac planned to start a music school in the region between Marseilles and Barcelona.

ALEXANDRE TANSMAN
(1897-1986)

Tansman was born in Łódź, Poland, but lived in France for most of his life. While in Poland he trained in music at the Łódź Conservatory and completed a doctorate in law at the University of Warsaw (1918). After moving to Paris in 1920, he met Stravinsky and Ravel, both of whom encouraged his work. Tansman found his way into the Ecole de Paris, a group of foreign musicians that included Bohuslav Martinů Tansman enjoyed international success, with his orchestral music performed under such esteemed conductors as Koussevitzky, Toscanini, and Stokowski. During an American concert tour as pianist with Koussevitzky and the Boston Symphony in 1927, Tansman met George Gershwin. His concertizing also took him to Europe, Asia, Palestine and India, where he was a guest of Mahatma Gandhi in 1933. He gained French citizenship in 1938, but because of his Jewish heritage, he and his family were soon forced to flee France to the United States. Settled in Los Angeles, Tansman became acquainted with Schoenberg and composed a number of film scores. He returned to Paris in 1946. His honors included the Coolidge Medal (1941), election to the Académie Royale of Belgium (1977) and the Polish Medal of Cultural Merit (1983). He composed hundreds of pieces in total, exploring practically every musical genre, from symphonies to ballets to chamber music and works for solo guitar.

POINTS FOR PRACTICE AND TEACHING

Yachting / *Le Yachting*
from Sports and Pastimes / *Sports et Divertissements*
Erik Satie

- Note the commentary; in typical fashion, Satie is telling an unconventional story. Remember not to read the story out loud, as the composer forbade it.
- Even though yachting would seem to be a relaxing activity, the narrative in the text depicts a cloudy day on which it might rain. The music is appropriately moody.
- This piece uses a repetitive sequence of four broken chords in the bass. In m. 1-4 and m. 17-20 the pattern is shared between the L.H. and R.H., and in m. 15-16 the R.H. doubles it two octaves higher, but otherwise the L.H. plays it alone.
- For this continuous pattern, relax the L.H. Use wrist rotation to help you reach the high and low notes.
- The R.H.'s constantly changing material may seem a bit random, but think of it as decoration over the bass accompaniment.

Polka / *Polka*
from The Villagers / *Villagoises*
Francis Poulenc

- This jaunty piece begins with a section marked "very dry". Keep the repeated notes in the R.H. short and crisp, and use no pedal.
- In m. 9, the mood changes drastically. The dynamic switches from *f* to *p*, and instead of sharp dry notes there are smooth *legato* phrases. Overemphasize this change of character.
- In m. 23 to the end, both hands have somewhat athletic gestures. The R.H. must expand to a ninth chord and then contract to play repeated notes. Meanwhile, the L.H. leaps between the treble clef and bass clef. Practice the hands separately and slowly!
- If you are unable to reach the ninth chords in the R.H., take the A-flats at the bottom of each chord with the L.H.

Gnossienne No. 3 / *Gnossienne No. 3*
from Three Gnossiennes / *Trois Gnossiennes*
Erik Satie

- This is one of Satie's darkest, most meditative pieces. The title *Gnossienne* may be a reference to *gnose* (*gnosis*, or personal/intellectual knowledge, the basis of the belief system of Gnosticism).
- Satie was known for eccentric indications, often more philosophical than musical, and this score contains some unusual instructions for the pianist. Do not overthink them, but instead try to react spontaneously as you play.
- Though the piece has no time signature or barlines, the beat remains the same throughout.
- The texture remains essentially the same throughout: short gestures and scalar motives in the R.H., and a bass accompaniment pattern of low notes followed by two chords.
- In system 10, the harmonic change to F minor is especially dark. Make this moment special.
- This piece has a wandering quality. To keep it focused and coherent, pay attention to the resolutions at the end of each wandering scale. For example, in system 4, lean into the low A bass note.
- At the very end of the piece, the music should seem to continue onward, without a definite conclusion. Try a slight *decrescendo* at the end.
- Use sustaining pedal in this piece. Start by changing the pedal on each L.H. whole note, and then modify as necessary.

The girl with the flaxen hair / *La fille aux cheveux de lin*
from Preludes, Book 1 / *Préludes, première livre*
Claude Debussy

- The top notes of the R.H. are the melody, and should be slightly brought out.
- Begin early practice at a slightly louder dynamic than *p*, to become secure in the music.
- Try to achieve as much *legato* as possible using the fingers only, without the sustaining pedal.
- Have the discipline to practice without sustaining pedal. Only when you have learned the piece well should you begin to add pedal.
- The most common mistake in playing Debussy is too much pedal. Keep the harmonies clear.
- Some spots require extra practice for most, including measures 24–27 and measure 35.
- In the third beat of measure 6 in the L.H., play the low E-flat and B-flat as sort of grace note before the beat, then the hand jumps up to play the higher G and B-flat.
- Debussy used the parallel slashes at the end of measure 11 to simply say that the "cédez" (a slowing of the tempo) ends. He did not intend a lifting of the hands. The same is true of measures 23 and 27.
- The climax is only *mf*. Keep it contained.

Rainy Day / *Jour de pluie*
from Ten Diversions for the Young Pianist / *Dix Récréations pour le jeune pianist*
Alexandre Tansman

- This beautiful, impressionistic piece evokes slow and steady rain.
- The R.H. plays the exact same pattern throughout the entire piece. Make sure to relax so that the hand can play the pattern steadily without becoming tense.
- Bring out the L.H. more, since the R.H. only has a repeated pattern.
- Note the many *tenuto* marking on L.H. chords. Some of these chords sound so beautiful against the R.H. pattern that you'll want to sink into them!
- In some places the L.H. plays a chord with open ties. This marking means to let the chord ring, holding it in the pedal while moving to a new chord.
- Find a reasonable tempo that allows you to play the chain of sixths in m. 5-6 smoothly. At the same time, do not drag too much.
- In m. 26, the L.H. has a rather fancy double fingering substitution. If you attempt this, make the switch on beat 2.

Rustic Piece / *Rustique*
from The Villagers / *Villagoises*
Francis Poulenc

- This piece brims with excitement. Poulenc's metronome mark is quite fast, and may not be possible for all players. As with most fast pieces, start practicing at a slow, manageable tempo.
- Some of the L.H. notes have been notated in the treble staff, probably because they sit in a range that would be harder to read in the bass clef. The R.H. plays just the top melody line throughout the piece; the only exception is in beats 3 and 4 of m. 8.
- Pay attention to the written phrasing; Poulenc has divided the melody line into short gestures that give it a breathless, excited quality.
- Use a round, rich tone in the restatement of the opening melody at m. 11. In an orchestra, this line might be played by cellos or bassoons.
- Poulenc has given only two dynamic markings: a *p* at the beginning and another *p* at m. 17.

The Child of the Troop / *L'Enfant de Troupe*
from Poetic Pieces, Book 2 / *Pièces poétiques, deuxième cahier*
Henri Sauguet

- This seems to be a portrait of a child in a military entourage. Sauguet dedicated the piece to Jean Alvarez de Toledo, a Spanish general.
- The overall character is a light march, with many grace notes in the melody.
- Considering the dry, *secco* nature of much of the piece, do not use any sustaining pedal except maybe to assist in *legato* playing in m. 14-20.
- Use a smooth back-and-forth motion of the L.H. to achieve a steady accompaniment in m. 1-5, m. 11-13, and elsewhere.
- The sixteenth-note runs in m. 14-17 require careful coordination. Practice hands separately to become comfortable with the fingering.
- M. 29-36 contain a sort of a variation of the opening melody. Keep a light touch in the R.H. to move through the string of *staccato* sixteenths without tension or accidental slurring.
- Pay attention to dynamic changes throughout. The piece is mostly set around a *p* dynamic; this child seems a bit shy.

The (Perpetual) Tango / *Le Tango - perpetual*
from Sports and Pastimes / *Sports et Divertissements*
Erik Satie

- The L.H. continuously plays a tango rhythm, a dance form from Argentina.
- Notice the whimsical commentary about the Devil dancing the tango to cool off.
- The R.H. is sometimes notated in up-stemmed notes in the bass staff, making the rhythmic relationship between hands clearer.
- Keep consistent articulations in the tango style: mostly *staccato* but with slurs on the sixteenths. Also aim for strong emphasis on beats 1 and 3 of each measure.
- Satie was not joking about this being a "perpetual" tango; the music ends with a repeat and can be played through as many times as you wish.

The Races / *Les Courses*
from Sports and Pastimes / *Sports et Divertissements*
Erik Satie

- From Satie's commentary, this piece appears to portray a horse race.
- The L.H.'s continuous *ostinato* (repeated melodic/rhythmic pattern at the same pitch) simulates running, and like running a race, you must pace yourself with a reasonable tempo to avoid fatigue.
- The C-sharp of the ostinato can be played with either the second or third finger of the L.H. Different players will find different fingerings more comfortable.
- The R.H.'s material from "Here come the losers" to the end may be an abstract quotation of "La Marseillaise," the tune for the French national anthem.
- Note the dynamic changes. In m. 2-3, the music *crescendos* from *p* to *f*. In m. 4 it suddenly drops down to *pp*. Observing these dramatic changes will give the music added character.

In Chapel / *Toto déguisé en Suisse d'église*
from On Vacation / *En vacances, 1er recueil*
Deodat de Séverac

- Séverac achieves a solemn, pious atmosphere by using some hymnlike textures.
- The pedal markings are the composer's.
- In m. 9-12, let the R.H.'s top melody sing while both hands provide accompaniment. When this happens again in m. 17-20, use the pedal carefully to create a *legato* sound while jumping to different octaves in the melody.
- The L.H. chord on beat 4 of m. 11 will probably need to be rolled except for those with very large hands.
- Follow all the dynamic swells from *p* to *mf* and then back to *p*.

First Act Prelude - The Calling / *Prélude du Premier Acte - La Vocation*
from The Son of the Stars / *Le Fils d'Étoiles*
Erik Satie

- Satie was commissioned to write incidental music for a three-act play called *The Son of the Stars*, which had some mystical undertones. This prelude comes from the score.
- The harmonies in the first three systems were very adventurous for their time. Try to keep the gestures distant and mysterious.
- Despite the lack of barlines, much of this piece is in conventional 4/4.
- In the fourth system, under the marking "Affectedly" (and its restatement in the second-to-last system), use the pedal to produce a *legato* sound in the melody in octaves. Octaves at this tempo should not be showy.
- The two sections in the piece marked *f*, under the text "Pale and hieratic" (pale and priestlike) should be played with a sense of grandeur, letting the chords ring out.
- The section beginning at the tempo **Avec calme** should be played steadily, without dragging. Feel the unusual resolutions of each pair of chords. The meditative, wandering quality of this music is quite hypnotic if executed properly.

Life / *la vie*
from A Child Loves / *L'Enfant Aime*
Darius Milhaud

- In a relatively short duration, this piece travels through many moods, motives, and harmonies. Milhaud deserves credit for attempting to portray life itself as part of his suite *A Child Loves*…
- The overall character is of a child exuberantly running from one activity to the next. Notice how the opening melody keeps returning as a fragment before the music abruptly switches to something else.
- Milhaud has written lots of details and articulations into this piece. Pay careful attention to these to create character.
- Several moments in the piece create syncopation through unusual placement of accents. Notice the accents in m. 11-13 and m. 48-50, and also m. 51-53.
- To process the variety of materials here, try breaking the piece into smaller sections. Here is one example breakdown:
- A: m. 1-13, B: m. 14-21, C: m. 22-29, D: m. 30-37, A1: m. 38-50, coda: m. 51-56.
- Even if you don't follow the smaller sections, it is important to recognize that m. 38-50 are a rough restatement of m. 1-13.

Rêverie / *Rêverie*

Claude Debussy

- Strive for a very delicate sound. See how beautiful you can make the R.H. melody beginning at m. 3.
- In m. 11 and onward, use gentle throws of the hand to navigate the L.H. arpeggios: from the thumb to the fifth finger in the first two beats of m. 11, to the fifth finger on beat 3 of m. 12, back down to the fifth finger on the downbeat of m. 13, etc. Don't try to reach, but use the wrist to get where you need to go.
- In m. 19-27, try for as *legato* a line as possible by keeping at least one voice legato from octave to octave. The stationary E-flat in the R.H. of mm. 19–21 acts as a pivot, allowing the hand to swing freely from octave to octave, and to get as many octaves as possible into one wrist gesture.
- In m. 27-30, have fun with the dynamic contrasts, creating two distinct characters between phrases.
- m. 48: The L.H. should take the final two eighth notes of this measure, lightly throwing from the C an octave beneath, and softly coloring the R.H. melody.
- m. 51: In pedaling these *portamento* chords, try to catch the note with the pedal while still touching the key before releasing your fingers.
- m. 56: The B on the fourth beat must be played gently since it begins an inner voice, and the principal melody starts on the following downbeat.
- mm. 76–82: Practice the melody that passes between the hands until a smooth transition using consistent fingering is achieved and beautifully shaped.
- m. 86 and following: Note the dynamic differences from the opening of the piece.

Speeding Along / *À toute vitesse*

from Ten Diversions for the Young Pianist / *Dix Récréations pour le jeune pianist*

Alexandre Tansman

- The constant flow of sixteenth notes and frequent hand position changes make slow practice essential.
- All notes should be played perfectly evenly.
- The L.H. part in m. 1-8 is a walking bass line that moves down by half step.
- Given the Bach-like nature of the piece, no sustaining pedal should be used.
- Certain sections in this piece repeat, making it friendlier than it may look on the page. M. 1-4 and m. 33-36 are the same, m. 9-11 and m. 13-15 are the same, and m. 17-20 and m. 21-24 are the same.
- The L.H. has another descending line in m. 17-20, repeated in m. 21-24.
- Make sure to observe articulations when the R.H. has *legato* runs over the L.H.'s *staccato* notes in m. 1-8 and m. 33-36.

The Cylists / *Les Cyclistes*

from Poetic Pieces, Book 1 / *Pièces poétiques, prèmiere cahier*

Henri Sauguet

- Keep the R.H.'s constant sixteenth notes steady and even.
- M. 1-6 and m. 19-24 are the same.
- In m. 11-12, the R.H. plays chords while the L.H. plays sixteenth notes. Then in m. 13-14 the hands swap textures.
- Notice that in the figures in m. 28-30, the L.H. plays the last note of each 4-note group.
- Start practicing slowly. As you master the piece, build to a tempo that lives up to **Vivo**.

Young Men Working / *Travaillez "Garçons"*
from Little Hands / *Petites mains*
Pierre Sancan

- The music moves rapidly through different scales, some of which defy standard major or minor labels. Pay careful attention to accidentals.
- Practice scales as you work on this piece.
- Sancan has purposefully written clashes between major and minor figures that create dissonance. Some notes may sound "wrong" in context, but this is his playful intention.
- Notice how the R.H. and L.H. often play the same gestures, but with the L.H. entering one bar late as an echo or imitation. This helps to evoke an image of workers handing each other equipment or collaborating on a task.
- Be sure to follow the *tenutos* as part of each gesture. If each *tenuto* is properly played from hand to hand, it will enhance the imitative effect.
- Since the piece is mostly made up of ascending scales, one might imagine these young men are working on a construction project!
- In m. 14-19, the motives change from scales to arpeggios. The L.H. arpeggios travel constantly upward, while the R.H. turns down briefly in each third beat.
- M. 23-30 are almost identical to m. 1-7 and may come as a relief after many twists and turns.
- Practice hands slowly and separately. The eighth notes must be absolutely steady and legato.

Toccata / *Toccata*
from Ten Diversions for the Young Pianist / *Dix Récréations pour le jeune pianist*
Alexandre Tansman

- This exciting finale has a lot in common with Tansman's own *Speeding Along* from earlier in this volume. An easy-to-follow L.H. part, once again descending by step, allows the player to give more attention to the challenges in the R.H.
- This particular type of figure in the R.H. is tempting to rush, but take time and make sure you master it at a slow tempo first.
- Keep the R.H. sixteenths *legato* and the L.H. eighths *staccato*.
- The R.H. figures outline chords and create implied harmonies.
- In m. 10-12, the texture changes so that the L.H. only plays on beats 1 and 3. Make sure to release the L.H. notes on the rests.
- In m. 12-15, Tansman uses a compositional technique called pedal bass, where the bottom note remains static while harmonies change above. This is often used to build tension and excitement before a conclusion. Though no dynamics are marked here, feel free to add some intensity!
- During the pedal bass section in m. 12-15, the L.H. begins a new pattern that involves constant leaps of a ninth. Keep the hand relaxed and light, without overly stretching to the top B-flats and B's.
- M. 16-23 are almost identical to m. 1-7.
- Successfully mastering this piece will prepare you for many other advanced pieces where the R.H. plays constant sixteenths without much of a break.

– Brendan Fox
editor

Yachting

from *Sports and Pastimes*

Erik Satie

Satie often included phrases of narrative text in his piano music. He forbade these to be read aloud during performance.

Can no one calm her down?

"I don't want to stay here,"

says the pretty passenger.

"It is not amusing.

I prefer something else.

legato

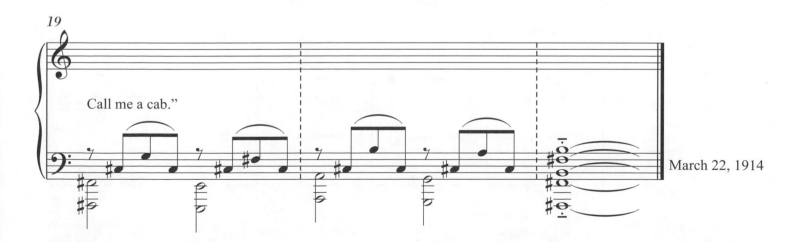

Call me a cab."

March 22, 1914

4

Polka
from *The Villagers*

Francis Poulenc

© 1933 Éditions SALABERT
Paris, France

Gnossienne No. 3

from *Three Gnossiennes*

Erik Satie

★This tie is not present in some publications.

© 1913 Éditions SALABERT
Paris, France

*Tous droits réservés
pour tous pays*

6

Carry this further away

Open the head

Muffle the sound

La fille aux cheveux de lin

from *Préludes*, Book 1

Claude Debussy
L. 117, No. 8

Très calme et doucement expressif [♩ = 66]

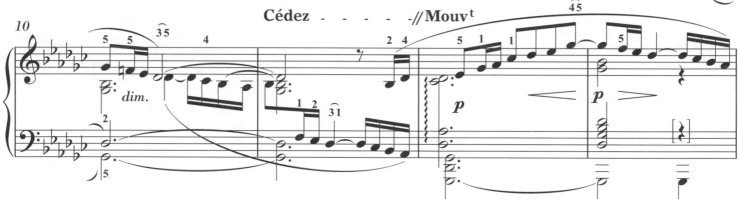

Fingerings are by the composer.

Rainy Day

from *Ten Diversions for the Young Pianist*

Alexandre Tansman

Lento [♩ = c. 64]

sempre legato

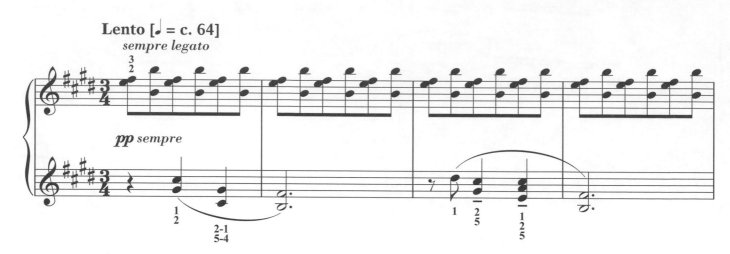

pp sempre

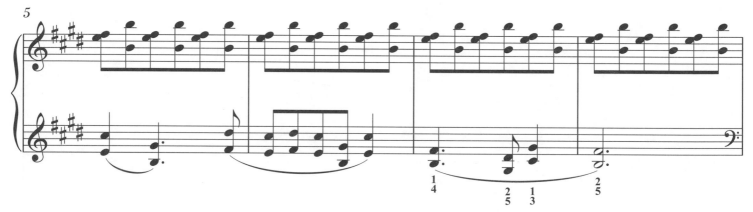

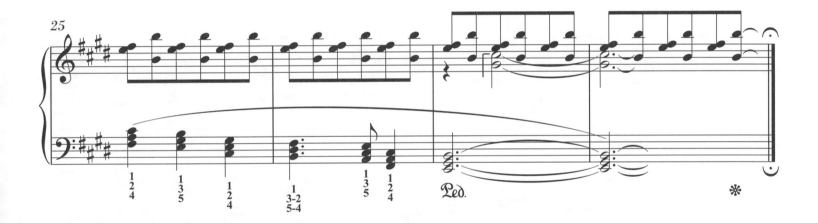

Rustic Piece

from *The Villagers*

Francis Poulenc

Vif et gai ♩ = 144

m. g. dessus *

* Even though this is Poulenc's marking, the editors recommend l.h. over r.h.

Jean Alvarez de Toledo

The Child of the Troop

from *Poetic Pieces*, Book 2

Henri Sauguet

Allegro moderato [♩ = c. 72]

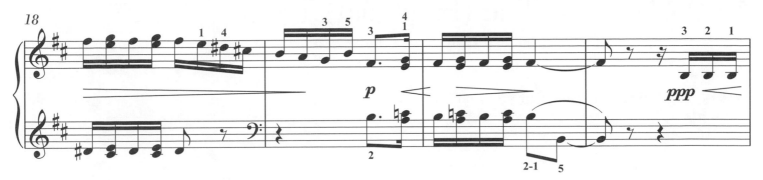

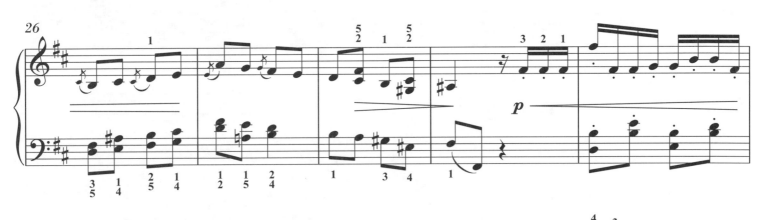

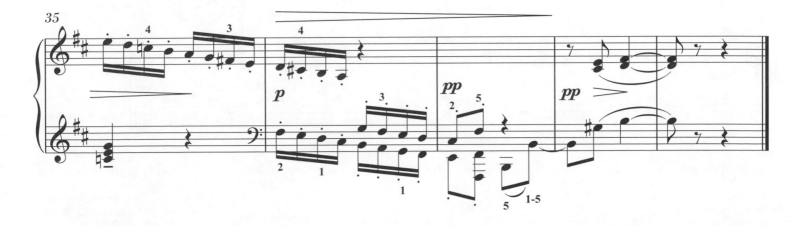

The (Perpetual) Tango

from *Sports and Pastimes*

Erik Satie

The tango is the Devil's dance.

His favorite one.

He uses it for cooling off.

His wife, his daughters, and his servants all cool off

that way.

May 5, 1914

Repeat as many times as you wish.

Satie often included phrases of narrative text in his piano music. He forbade these to be read aloud during performance.

The Races
from *Sports and Pastimes*

Erik Satie

Satie often included phrases of narrative text in his piano music. He forbade these to be read aloud during performance.

In Chapel

from *On Vacation*, Volume 1

Déodat de Séverac

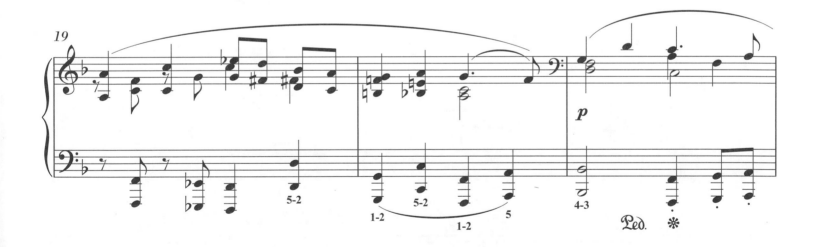

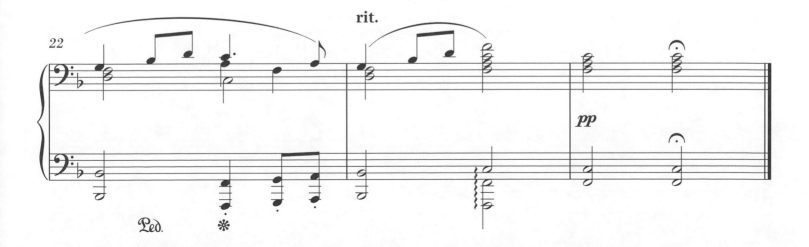

First Act Prelude - The Calling

from *The Son of the Stars*

Erik Satie

This is Satie's original notation, without meter or barlines.

Avec calme
Like a gentle question

Always

Affectedly

Pale and hieratic

Life
from *A Child Loves*

Darius Milhaud

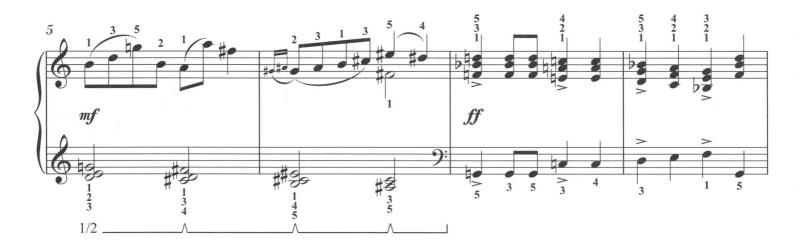

24

Rêverie

Claude Debussy
L. 68

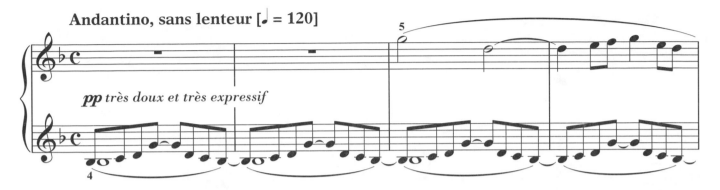

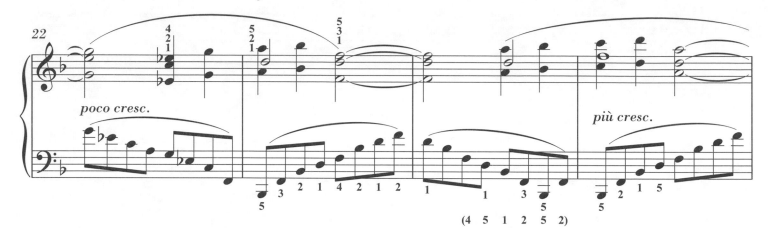

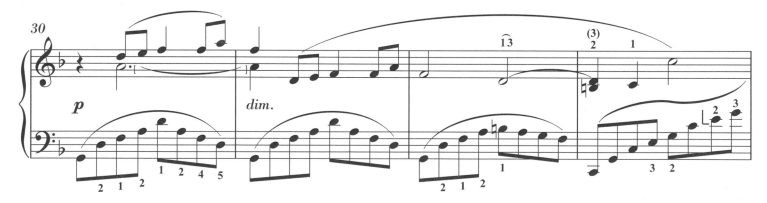

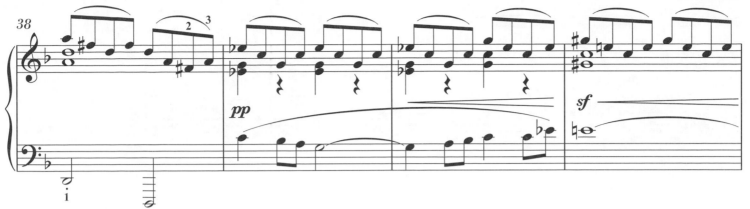

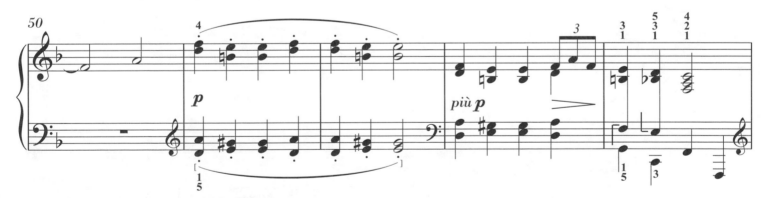

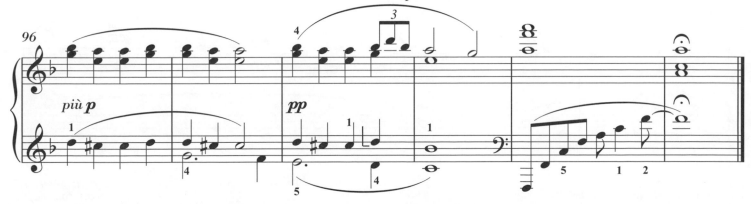

Speeding Along

from *Ten Diversions for the Young Pianist*

Alexandre Tansman

Allegro vivace [♩ = c. 92]

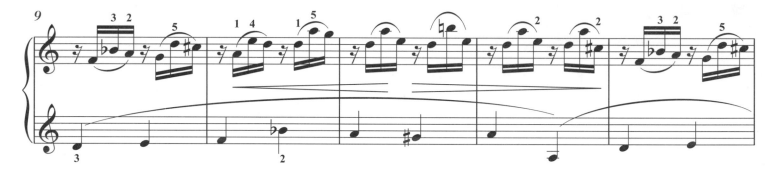

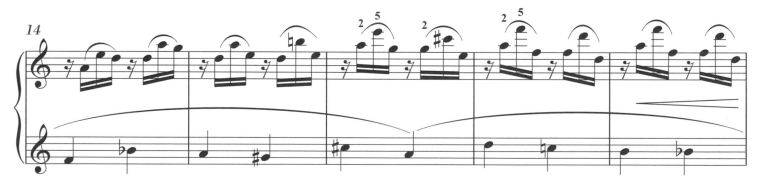

à Lucie Noreno

The Cyclists

from *Poetic Pieces*, Book 1

Henri Sauguet

Tous droits réservés
pour tous pays

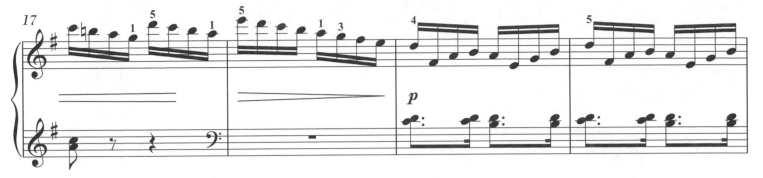

Young Men Working

from *For Small Hands*

Pierre Sancan

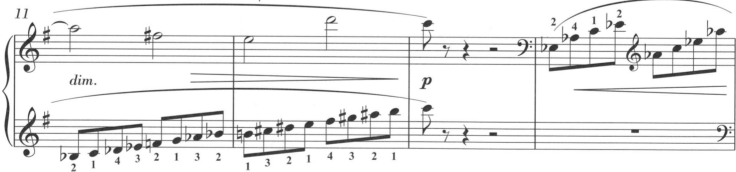

Tous droits réservés
pour tous pays

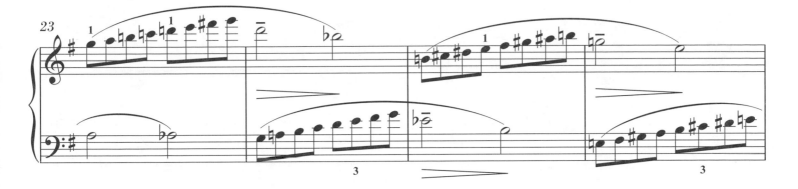

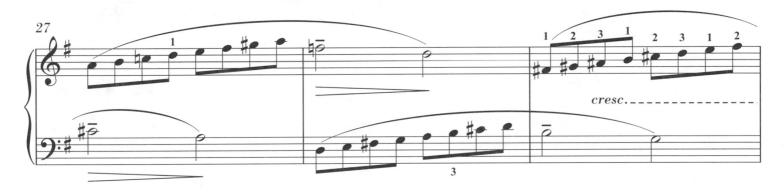

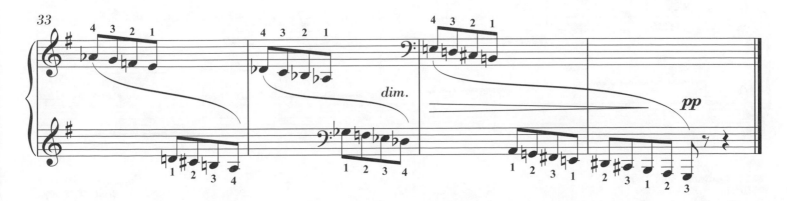

Toccata

from *Ten Diversions for the Young Pianist*

Alexandre Tansman

Vivace [♩ = c. 96]

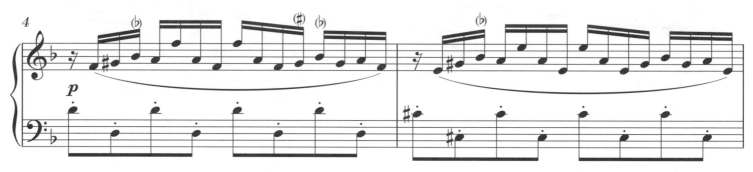

GLOSSARY OF FRENCH MUSICAL TERMS

au mouvt. (retour au mouvement)	*return to tempo*
avec calme	*calmly*
cédez	*slow down*
m.g. (main gauche) dessus	*left hand under*
modéré	*moderately*
modéré et très ennuyé	*moderately and very restless*
murmuré et en retenant peu à peu	*murmuring and holding back little by little*
sans hâte	*without haste*
sans lenteur	*without dragging*
sans lourdeur	*without heaviness*
sans pédale	*without pedal*
sans ralentir	*without slowing down*
sans rigeur	*without rigor*
sec	*dry*
très anime	*very animated*
très calme et doucement expressif	*very calm and gently expressive*
très doux et très expressif	*very soft and very expressive*
très lié	*very connected*
très peu	*very slightly*
très sec	*very dry*
un peu animé	*a bit animated*
un peu retenu	*a little held back*
un peu vif	*somewhat fast*
vif et gai	*lively and cheerful*